Bold Expansion
The Nelson-Atkins Museum of Art
Bloch Building

The Nelson-Atkins
Museum of Art
in association with
Scala Publishers

SCALA

"The soul has greater need of the ideal than of the real."
Victor Hugo

Carved on the south façade of The Nelson-Atkins Museum of Art

This book is dedicated to the craftsmen,
designers, artisans, laborers, staff, volunteers
and community members whose commitment
to the ideal made this project real.

Contents

Foreword   4

A Refounding Begins   6

An International Search   12

A Creative Vision   16

Transformation of a Classic   22

Foreword

EACH OF US WILL experience the Museum's new Bloch Building in our own way. We will find new ways to make sense of an unfamiliar architecture, one that does not adhere to traditional formal organization and symbolic meaning. After all, how do you come to grips with a building that is 840 feet long, no more than 100 feet wide, has no front, no back and plays hide-and-seek like a chameleon with the landscape around it?

Nothing in the architecture or in the installation of the art is a matter of chance or whimsy. Intervals of space and time create a dynamic of elasticity that is rarely found in other buildings. If nothing is a matter of chance, then it is fair to ask: What is driving what we see? From the outside, we first notice that it is impossible to comprehend the building and how it is constructed from one vantage point or even from multiple vantage points.

Historically, buildings in the West have been conceived as coherent, relatively compact masses. A perfect example is the Nelson-Atkins Building itself, a well-defined, visually self-sufficient mass sitting on a hill, not engaging its surroundings spatially or visually. It dominates by

DIRECTOR/CEO
Marc F. Wilson, the Menefee D. &
Mary Louise Blackwell Director/CEO
of The Nelson-Atkins Museum of Art

Following Pages
DUAL REFLECTIONS
Viewed from the north, the Bloch
Building is a serene complement to
the formal Nelson-Atkins Building.

being king of the mountain. By contrast, Steven Holl's building has no façade, no back, not even a face that governs general orientation. It reads not as a single mass but as large, irregular glass sculptures with variable, shifting visual aspects that deny a quick, easy identification of relationships and function. As you attempt to sort out what you see, no shape lets you infer what lies on its other side. Have you ever been invited by a building to have an active, flowing, three-dimensional relationship with it?

To the purely visual experience, Holl has added kinesthetic sensations felt as we move through spaces in and among the glass-sculpture pavilions. If the eye is never allowed to comprehend the whole of the building, our other senses are given the treat of sensing spaces grow, become, morph and change. Space is not homogeneous. It is elastic. It is like putty, to be stretched, pulled and compressed. All the while, your mind is torn between the knowledge that you are moving through a built environment where there is no separation between the architecture and the outer landscape. The site is the building, but then the building is the site.

As you skip from picture to picture in the following pages, you will be reminded that the experience of the interior is governed by many of the same architectural principles as the exterior treatment, not in service of surrounding landscape but of the Museum's overarching goal of constructing an architectural environment that encourages a rich, meaningful dialogue between visitors and works of art Holl's design brilliantly declares that a forcefully artistic building can serve the art within it sympathetically. Ceilings fold and tilt. Walls kink. Views and planes crisscross. Spaces flow, changing – never repeating a shape. Despite the dynamic rhythms of light, planes and intervals, the pervading feeling is calm. None of this is mere architectural artistry for its own sake.

It all comes down to providing our visitors with the most rewarding experience of works of art; this amounts to the genius of one extraordinary individual affecting the sensibilities and emotional compass of another.

Time and history will have the final say about whether or not we have been successful. This project has been a remarkable coming together of firmly held values and a clear sense of purpose embraced by all.

Marc F. Wilson

A Refounding Begins

FROM ITS INCEPTION, The Nelson-Atkins Museum of Art was intended to inspire and enrich the growing community of Kansas City. The neoclassical building, sitting majestically on a grand lawn, opened to the public in 1933. As the 20th century progressed, the Nelson-Atkins' encyclopedic collection grew rapidly, and the Museum gained international stature for its remarkable Asian holdings. The Kansas City community developed a deep affection for the Museum, which became firmly established in the cultural fabric of the region.

In 1993, when the Nelson-Atkins passed its 60-year anniversary, Museum trustees and director Marc F. Wilson realized they were at an important juncture. The Museum had reached a plateau on every level—conceptually, intellectually and emotionally—and the time had come to fundamentally rethink the institution's future.

The 1990s will be remembered as a time of refounding for the Nelson-Atkins. Through extensive research, surveys of the community, retreats with staff and consultants, Museum leaders asked the most important questions: How could the visitors' experience with art become even more meaningful? What needs were not being met? How could the Museum reach further into the community, to enrich and educate, to bring more people into the fold of the Nelson-Atkins?

What came out of this measured process, which was truly years in the making, was a well-reasoned plan for the transformation of the entire Museum. At the heart of the vision was the desire to reach out to the community and region, to satisfy visitors' interest in seeing more works of art and getting more out of the collection.

As part of this refounding, it became clear that the Nelson-Atkins was woefully cramped, and leaders embraced the need for expansion. They did not set out to build a building, but rather to create a strategic roadmap for the future, continuing the founders' original vision of planning for growth. A building expansion was simply one outcome of the overall transformation of the Nelson-Atkins.

Clearly, this was a difficult task. Icons are not easily altered, especially classic buildings. The original trustees had the foresight to plan for the future, so that when the Nelson-Atkins opened in 1933, works of art filled only half of the first floor. The entire west wing was an empty, hollow shell void of rooms. By 1949, the west wing first floor

WORKING DRAWING
The Nelson-Atkins south façade in a 1929 architectural drawing.

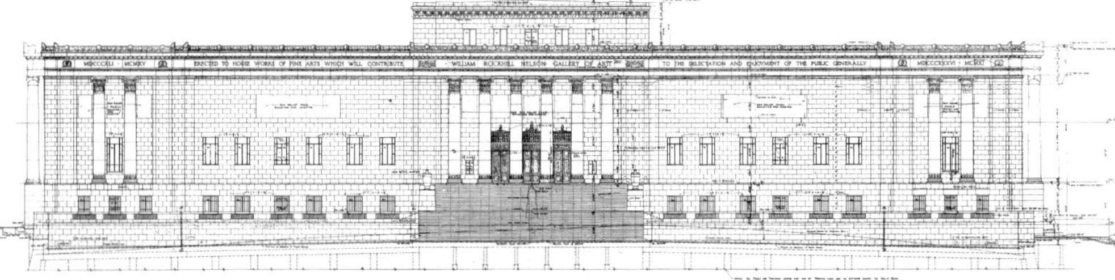

opened and by 1976, the second floor of the west wing opened. But by
the 1990s, the collection had outgrown the walls of the Museum.

Adding on to the architecturally pristine building was seen as such
an intriguing problem that the Nelson-Atkins expansion was often used
as a project for architecture students at area universities. Through the
years, Wilson had seen a wide range of plans, from separate buildings
to expansions that mirrored the original, from Sphinx-like structures
that extended into the south lawn to an admired extension to the north
that created an inner courtyard.

The original architects, Wight & Wight, left behind a drawing with
dotted lines, suggesting the addition of straight wings projecting north
from the east and west ends of the existing building. The Beaux-Arts
building was the embodiment of architecture as it was envisioned in
the 1930s. But as part of the 21st-century transformation of the Nelson-
Atkins, the new expansion was to be of its time, both in materials and in
architecture.

The expansion was the first fundamental change to the Nelson-
Atkins Building, and it was understood and clearly stated that the
expansion was to be a significant contribution to architecture as well as
a home for distinguished works of art. Most importantly, the expansion
was to function as a Museum.

After detailed evaluation of existing square footage throughout the
Museum, an architectural program was designed that spelled out
precise requirements for the new building. The program, developed by
Boston-based E. Verner Johnson and Associates, was based on careful
analysis of relationships between one department and another. Every
element of the Museum expansion was outlined including specific
requirements for gallery space, offices, parking spaces, art storage, art
preparation, an art receiving dock, expanded library stacks, new
Museum Café and Store, and more.

STATELY PRESENCE
The Nelson-Atkins opened in 1933
and soon became a cultural icon
in the Midwest.

Following Pages
SOUTHERN FACADE
Fall colors highlight the south side of
the grand Nelson-Atkins Building.

IDEAL THAN
WILLIAM ROCKHILL NELSON GALLERY OF ART
THAT WE EXIST

An International
Search

BY LATE 1998, the Nelson-Atkins leaders had begun an international search for a world-renowned architect. They were looking for someone who had shown the ability to design innovative projects that were ultimately timeless. The chairman of the Museum's Board of Trustees was Donald J. Hall, chairman of Hallmark Cards Inc. and an extraordinary champion of the Nelson-Atkins. He possessed a passion for architecture and an aptitude for reading plans and visualizing their final constructed outcome. He assumed the role of chairman of the Architect Selection Committee.

For members of the committee, Hall pulled together an impressive group of people with strong reputations in the international world of architecture. Bill Lacy, president of Purchase College and executive director of the prestigious Pritzker Architecture Prize, architecture's highest honor, provided valued counsel to the committee.

Members of the committee, in addition to Hall and Wilson, were the late J. Carter Brown, director emeritus of the National Gallery of Art and chairman of the Pritzker Architecture Prize; Ada Louise Huxtable, the respected author and *Wall Street Journal* architecture critic; John C. Gaunt, dean of the School of Architecture and Urban Design at the University of Kansas. Vicki L. Noteis, an architect and director of planning and development for the city of Kansas City, was also a member of the committee. From the community, the committee included Henry W. Bloch, chairman of H&R Block Inc. and a Museum trustee; Arthur S. Brisbane, then president and publisher of *The Kansas City Star*, which shares a mutual founder with the Museum in William Rockhill Nelson; and Kathleen Collins, president of the nearby Kansas City Art Institute.

The committee's work was administered by Cary Goodman, then a principal of Gould Evans Goodman Associates. William H. Dunn Sr., chairman of the J. E. Dunn Construction Company, which would later construct the building, also was on hand as an advisor.

In January 1999, the committee began in earnest reviewing the work and qualifications of dozens of architects internationally. Ultimately, the list was whittled to six outstanding finalists.

It included Machado and Silvetti Associates, a Boston firm led by Rodolfo Machado and Jorge Silvetti, who both taught at Harvard and had received the American Academy of Arts and Letters, first Architecture Prize in 1991. They had been lauded for their design of the Robert F. Wagner Jr. Park in Battery Park City, New York.

Christian de Portzamparc of France, 1994 winner of the Pritzker Architecture Prize, was also a finalist. His City of Music project in Paris had been celebrated across Europe, and his sleek Louis Vuitton tower in New York was under construction. Japanese architect Tadao Ando, 1995 winner of the Pritzker Architecture Prize, was also included. His projects had largely been in Japan, but in the United States, he had designed the Modern Art Museum in Fort Worth, Texas.

Previous pages
SATURATED COLORS
Looking north, a rich evening view from atop the Bloch Building.

GOOD COMPANY
Architect Steven Holl was one of six
outstanding finalists chosen to submit
ideas for the expansion.

The list also included Steven Holl, a New York architect whose
work was international in scope, with projects from Japan to New
Mexico. He had gained notice for his asymmetrical Kiasma Museum
of Contemporary Art in Helsinki, Finland. Also among the finalists
were Carlos Jimenez of Houston, a professor at Rice University known
for his designs of urban educational facilities, including a new educa-
tion building for the Museum of Fine Arts in Houston. Finally, the list
included Annette Gigon and Mike Guyer, Swiss architects who had
designed the elegant Kirchner Museum in Davos, Switzerland.

The six architects came to Kansas City in April 1999 for a two-day
orientation, with remarks from committee members about the possibilities for the Nelson-Atkins. The expansion was to achieve more
space for an array of Museum needs, as outlined in the rigorous architectural program, and it was to be a building that would inspire generations. Wilson stressed to the finalists that function and economic
efficiency were paramount.

The architects were each given a large, black-bound book that they
were to fill over the next two months. Committee members wanted to
see two-dimensional presentations rather than models. The architects
were not given a hard directive that they should design an extension
to the north of the original building, but the implication was certainly
there, and it had been a long-held mindset that this was the preferred
location. It was understood that the sweeping view of the Nelson-
Atkins from the south should not be altered, and by default, the north
side had been on people's minds for years.

"The SOUL HAS GREATER NEED of
THE IDEAL Than of THE RE[AL]
FACADE inscription carve[d]
IN limeStone

The STONE & The FEATHER
HEAVY ——————— LIGHT
1933 ——————— 2002
Directed circulation ——— open circulation
BOUNDED ——————— UNBOUNDED
INWARD views ——————— VIEWS out into
LANDSCAPE
Hermetic — — — — — MESHING of inte[rior]
and EXTERIOR
Imported Indigenous

LANDSCAPE Views
NOGUCHI court

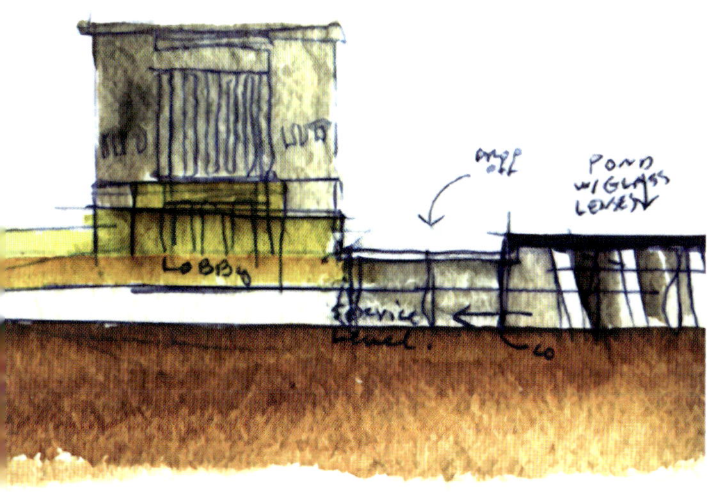

A Creative Vision

STEVEN HOLL had been to Kansas City and to the Nelson-Atkins in years past, but when he visited again in 1999, he viewed the site as an intriguing architectural project. He wandered through the Museum's world-renowned Asian collection, and was caught by a particular painting by Zhou Chen, *The North Sea,* from the Ming Dynasty (1368–1644). The silk handscroll features a secluded scholar's retreat on a hillside, partly hidden and partly seen through the rocks and foliage. Holl would return mentally to that image again as he thought about fusing architecture and landscape.

Holl walked the site and was struck by the potential of engaging the landscape of the Kansas City Sculpture Park. Rather than a single addition competing with the neoclassical building, he conceptualized multiple forms creating new spaces and viewpoints in the Sculpture Park. He quickly understood the difficulty of an expansion, of infringing on the perfect geometry of the original building and its situation on the site. His immediate impulse was not to build against the original structure, but to create a spatial relationship between the massive stone building and a new lighter building. He felt the site called for a new building rather than an addition. Just as the Acropolis' pavilions create courts which mask and reveal vistas of the Parthenon, the Nelson-Atkins expansion could be formed of pavilions shaping intervals of space with oblique views of the neoclassical building.

INSPIRED WORK
During his visit to the Nelson-Atkins, Holl was captured by this silk handscroll by Zhou Chen.

Zhou Chen, Chinese (1455–1536). *The North Sea* (detail), Ming Dynasty (1368–1644). Handscroll; ink and watercolor on silk. Purchase: Nelson Trust, 58-55.

STONE AND FEATHER
Steven Holl's sketches and
watercolors of a proposed expansion
were inspired by the grandness of the
original building. In an early sketch
(previous pages), he compared the
Nelson-Atkins to a stone and the
proposed expansion to a feather.

During that visit, Holl made his first sketch. A black mass
represented the original building, while long rays of yellow and brown
represented the new. A quick sketch of small oval shapes to the east
side of the campus hinted of plans yet to come. A building should not
be an object to behold, in Holl's words, but rather a series of spaces and
vistas that open and close. The way the sunlight hits the wall, the way
trees throw their shadows on the surface, the way the body moves
through the building, these are part of what Holl calls the "enmeshed
experience of architecture."

As the weeks went by, Holl and the other architects worked on their
notebooks of ideas while members of the committee set out to
personally see works designed by the six finalists, traveling nationally
and internationally.

In late June, each of the architects returned to Kansas City to make
a two-hour presentation to the selection committee. Four of the six
presented designs that made use of the north side of the Museum,
which at that time was primarily a parking area, and one firm presented
a series of possible solutions, including designs on the north side.

Steven Holl and project architect Chris McVoy made their
presentation last. Holl started by showing drawings of predictable
expansions to the north of the Nelson-Atkins, but explained that such a
mass would forever hide the original building. A northern expansion

SKY VIEW
Looking south, this aerial photograph of the transformed Museum shows Steven Holl's innovative use of the east side of the Nelson-Atkins campus.

would rob the opportunity to activate the south side of the building, he said, and would lose any connection with the Kansas City Sculpture Park. He described his vision of a building to the east side of the Nelson-Atkins Building, with an elongated design that was partly submerged in the landscape, partly visible in a series of glass "lenses." Rather than an expansion, his design would be a new building that would merge the lenses with the landscape, much the same way the structures merged with the hillside in the Zhou Chen painting.

Holl offered a description of complementary contrasts between the original building and his new concept. The strong neoclassic building was "stone" and his design was "feather." The original was "heavy" and the new was "light." The old was "hermetic and inward" and the new was "meshing," with outward views to the surrounding landscape.

Committee members began to understand just how Holl's design would work, how it would unfold to the side of the limestone building, how grass rooftops between the lenses would allow visitors to walk on top of the galleries to find new vistas of the Kansas City Sculpture Park and the original building. Holl talked of creating a unique translucent glass to form the exterior of the building. Committee members saw how the building would become a glowing, living structure at night when lit from within. As Holl and McVoy continued, committee members were intrigued by the possibilities, how breaking down the mass into smaller pavilions, or lenses, would not compete with the original building.

When the team had finished its presentation, committee members gathered to make their decision. Traditionally, the process of choosing from a cast of stellar architects would have gone into the night. But there was little discussion. The decision was so clear that the committee chose Steven Holl in less than 30 minutes. Holl's vision had reshaped the collective vision on how to expand Kansas City's cultural icon.

The groundbreaking took place in 2001, the same year Holl was named "America's best architect" by *Time* magazine. As construction began, Museum leaders recognized additional opportunities to improve the existing building and greatly expanded the scope of the original project. The original Nelson-Atkins Building was transformed with cleaning and tuck-pointing on the exterior, a new roof, improved mechanical systems, a new sculpture hall and the restoration and cleaning of Kirkwood Hall. Major projects were celebrated as they were completed, including an underground parking garage, new Ford Learning Center, transformed galleries, a reinstalled Kansas City Sculpture Park, and finally, the opening of the Bloch Building.

Transformation
of a Classic

Previous pages
TRANSFORMATION
The original building is reflected in
the clear glass of the Bloch Building.

FROM ANY VANTAGE POINT on campus, it is clear that the Nelson-Atkins has been dramatically transformed. On the north side, the change is especially dramatic. The classic façade has taken on a new elegance, underscored by the luminous Bloch Building to the east and the reflecting pool to the north. Steven Holl designed the pool as a unifying element for the Nelson-Atkins and the Bloch Building, with their reflections shining simultaneously in the water. He collaborated with the American artist Walter De Maria to create *One Sun / 34 Moons*, a domed bronze-and-steel slab covered in textured gold leaf, representing the sun rising out of the water. It is surrounded by 34 occuli, or lit lenses, encircled by white neon rings at the bottom of the pool, which signify the moons. The 34 glass portals on the bottom of the pool are also circular skylights that refract light and cast dancing figures of light onto the floor of the parking garage below.

From that serene north entrance, visitors can choose to go up the steps to the former main entrance of the Nelson-Atkins Building, which continues to be open to the public. Inside, the refurbished Kirkwood Hall remains as the Museum's grand ceremonial hall. Visitors find the elegant Adelaide Cobb Ward Sculpture Hall, which represents a connecting area, to be the physical and emotional heart between the historic and new buildings. They also find newly installed European galleries, with connections made between decorative arts, paintings, furniture, and sculptures. On the lower level of the building, they find the Ford Learning Center, with a collection of new studio classrooms, an innovative Educator Resource Center, and new access to the East Sculpture Terrace. The second floor continues to exhibit the Museum's world-class Asian collection, and visitors can look forward to the future reinstallation of the American collection and new American Indian galleries. The transformation within the Nelson-Atkins reaches every corner of the building.

Back outside at the granite-paved north J. C. Nichols Plaza, visitors are also welcomed by the new Bloch Building, named for Henry W. and Marion H. Bloch, whose dedication and vision helped transform the Nelson-Atkins. Here they can experience their first close-up look at the remarkable glass structure. The color of the building can vary widely, reflecting the light differently each hour of the day depending on the weather, the position of the sun, and the shade cast by the original building or nearby trees. Brooding blues, greens and grays give way to warm pinks, oranges and yellows as the sun rises and sets. What appears to be pure white to the eye glimmers across the surface of the lenses as the light of the day progresses.

REFLECTING POOL
Walter De Maria's minimalist
sculpture *One Sun / 34 Moons* is
on the north side of the campus.

BY DAY
Lens one of the Bloch Building is
reflected in the water. To the left, on
the north side of lens one, emerges
the vivid orange sculpture *Rumi*
by Mark di Suvero.

SHIFTING HUES
The glass of the Bloch Building reflects
the changing seasons of Kansas City.

ALL PASSES HIGH ART ALONE IS ETERNA

EASTERN FACADE
Seen from Rockhill Road along the east edge of the campus, the original Nelson-Atkins Building is framed by lenses one and two of the Bloch Building.

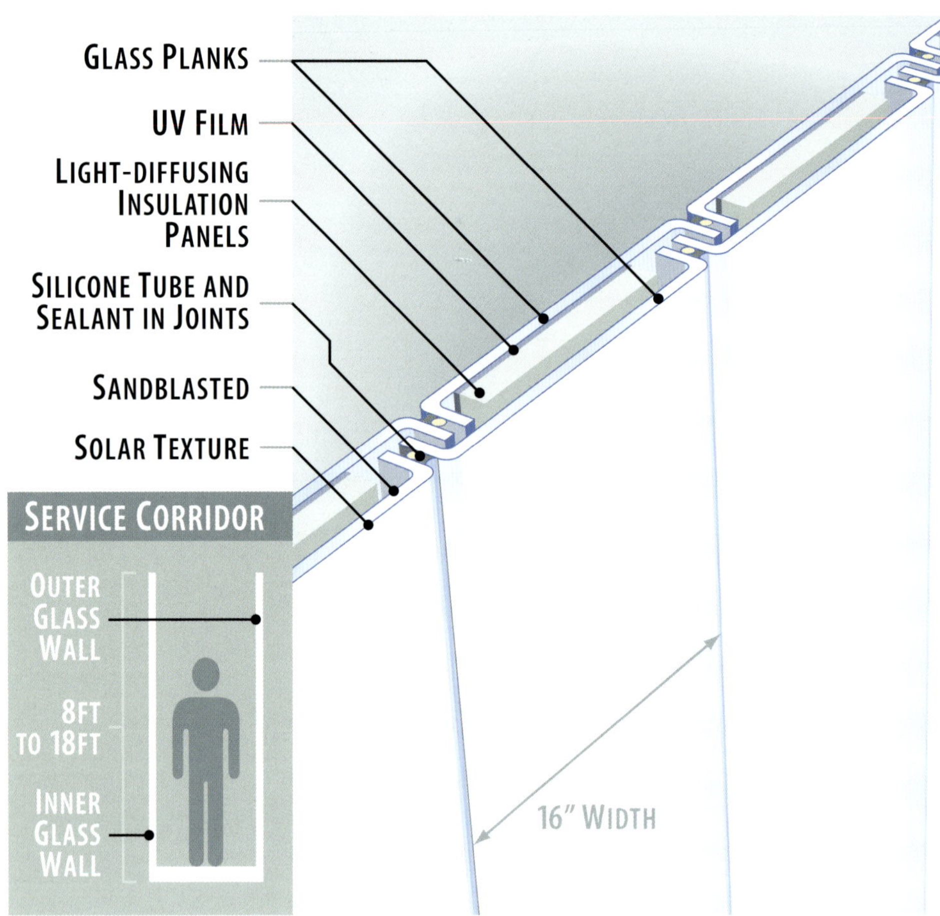

Extraordinary innovation led to the 16-inch glass planks, ranging in height from eight to 18 feet, that now shape the five lenses of Holl's design. The channel glass, manufactured by Lamberts Glasfabrik in Wunsiedel-Holenbrunn, Germany, was tested extensively before the more than 6,000 final planks were produced. Low iron content accounts for the near absence of green from the glass; solar rolling and sandblasting of the plank surface help diffuse the light. The system for installing the glass was developed in the United States specifically for the Nelson-Atkins. Exterior walls were created by sandwiching together the planks of U-shaped channel glass. A service corridor is tucked between the exterior walls of glass and interior walls.

UNIQUE DESIGN

The planks of glass are capped at the top and bottom by aluminum rails that expand and contract with the seasons.

SKYWARD
The two buildings contrast with
and complement one another.

Holl's use of light is one of the most important elements of the
Bloch Building. On sunny days, the light reflects, bends and refracts off
the multiple layers of glass, giving the building an opalescent glint. At
night, when the interior cavity is lit, the building glows with a soft
luminescence. The lenses at night have been compared to Japanese
lanterns or jewels that have been scattered down the eastern edge of
the lawn.

Wilson has said that the Nelson-Atkins Building immediately makes
itself clear as an important, civic structure. The Bloch Building, by
contrast, does not make a symbolic statement about its meaning or
function. The five lenses do not reveal that inside, an enormous 840-
foot-long building is submerged in the earth, the equivalent of a 67-
story structure laid on its side. The surprise of the Bloch Building, then,
begins when visitors walk through the door.

RADIANCE
(Above) The Bloch Building seen
at night along Rockhill Road.
(Right) Looking north from inside
the Kansas City Sculpture Park.

EVENING DRAMA
The evening sky accentuates
the drama of the north side of the
Nelson-Atkins.

Entering the building is a matter of choosing to go in from the granite-paved plaza level or the garage level. The garage was conceived as an entrance area, recognizing that the majority of Museum visitors will enter through the garage. Its distinctive ceiling features undulating vaults made of pre-cast concrete, and light shining through the reflecting pool above shimmers throughout the garage. Visitors enter through a lobby, passing the Museum Store and moving toward the central information area.

From the plaza level, visitors who come through the revolving doors will encounter the stunning grand stair, a slow rise of steps that appears to float. Before them, the first lens unfolds in layers of light and glass. The effect is powerful, an expansiveness that is achieved with soaring spaces and intriguing bends and lines of the architecture. Although the movement of the building is provocative and exciting, it emanates a feeling of calm. It is possible to stand in several places of the building and count nine or 10 shades of white and gray and color in one area of ceiling or wall. The planks of glass create vertical lines that are predictable and mathematical, but Steven Holl's walls, corridors and floors create abstract, surprising geometric patterns.

MOVING INSIDE

(Above) Light from portals in the plaza-level reflecting pool shines below into the award-winning garage. (Right) The Bloch Building's lines pull visitors toward the central lobby.

Visitors are visually drawn down an expansive ramp toward the central lobby space. However, some may venture up the grand stair where a corridor of exposed beams draws them to the Spencer Art Reference Library reading room, a quiet space lined with wooden bookshelves. The room is infused with light filtered through the translucent planks of glass.

The elegant staircase creates a dramatic angle in the entry to the Bloch Building.

LIGHT AND SHADOWS
Looking north in lens one, light falls
on the bends and folds of the Bloch
Building interior.

VIEW OF THE CALDER
Tom's Cubicle sits just outside the
central lobby of the Bloch Building.

Alexander Calder, American
(1898–1976). *Tom's Cubicle*, 1967.
Painted steel. Gift of the Friends of
Art, F69-7.

As visitors arrive in the central lobby, it is at once warm with the familiar and promising of the new. Here is where past and present meet in the most intimate and unobtrusive fashion. To the right is an actual portion of the Nelson-Atkins east façade, rough to the touch, with its warm golden hue, and the original Beaux-Arts light fixtures. Through the bronze doors that depict the story of *Hiawatha* are steps that lead into the majestic Adelaide Cobb Ward Sculpture Hall and the Nelson-Atkins Building. Visitors can look east, out the glass, to see Calder's black sculpture *Tom's Cubicle*. In this lobby area, the floor is of black terrazzo, embedded with sparkling glass chips, which contrasts sharply with the plaster walls, hand-applied with trowels and polished to a mottled sheen.

Choices abound in this area of connection, where visitors are able to interact with the Visitor Services Desk, pick up an audio guide or use a kiosk to locate a work of art or purchase an exhibition ticket. South doors beckon to the East Sculpture Terrace and offer the promise of the tranquil Kansas City Sculpture Park. Tall glass doors draw visitors into the first of the Bloch Building galleries.

BUILDINGS MEET
Original construction meets new construction in the visitors lobby of the Bloch Building, where the stone east façade of the Nelson-Atkins Building has been incorporated into the design.

The Bloch Building displays contemporary art, with works that were created after 1945, plus photography and African art. The featured exhibition spaces will host all types of art.

From north to south, the contemporary William T. Kemper Galleries are arranged in chronological order from the 1940s to the present. An area called Project Space shows the work of today's artists from around the world. Nearby a dazzling glass case displays works of world-renowned contemporary ceramic artists.

As visitors move further into the building, they find the canopy walls that curve dramatically outward at the top. Some end in midair; others soar to the glass of the lenses and bring differing qualities of light to their curved undersides. In many galleries, floors are of end-grain pattern oak, stained to a soft ebony.

EXPANSIVE VIEW

At the top of the grand stair, a meeting room features an impressive view of Rockhill Road, stretching toward the University of Missouri-Kansas City campus, and of a grassy area between the lenses and the Kansas City Sculpture Park.

VERTICAL DRAMA

Steven Holl's gallery designs include soaring canopies that draw the eye upward toward natural light.

Contemporary

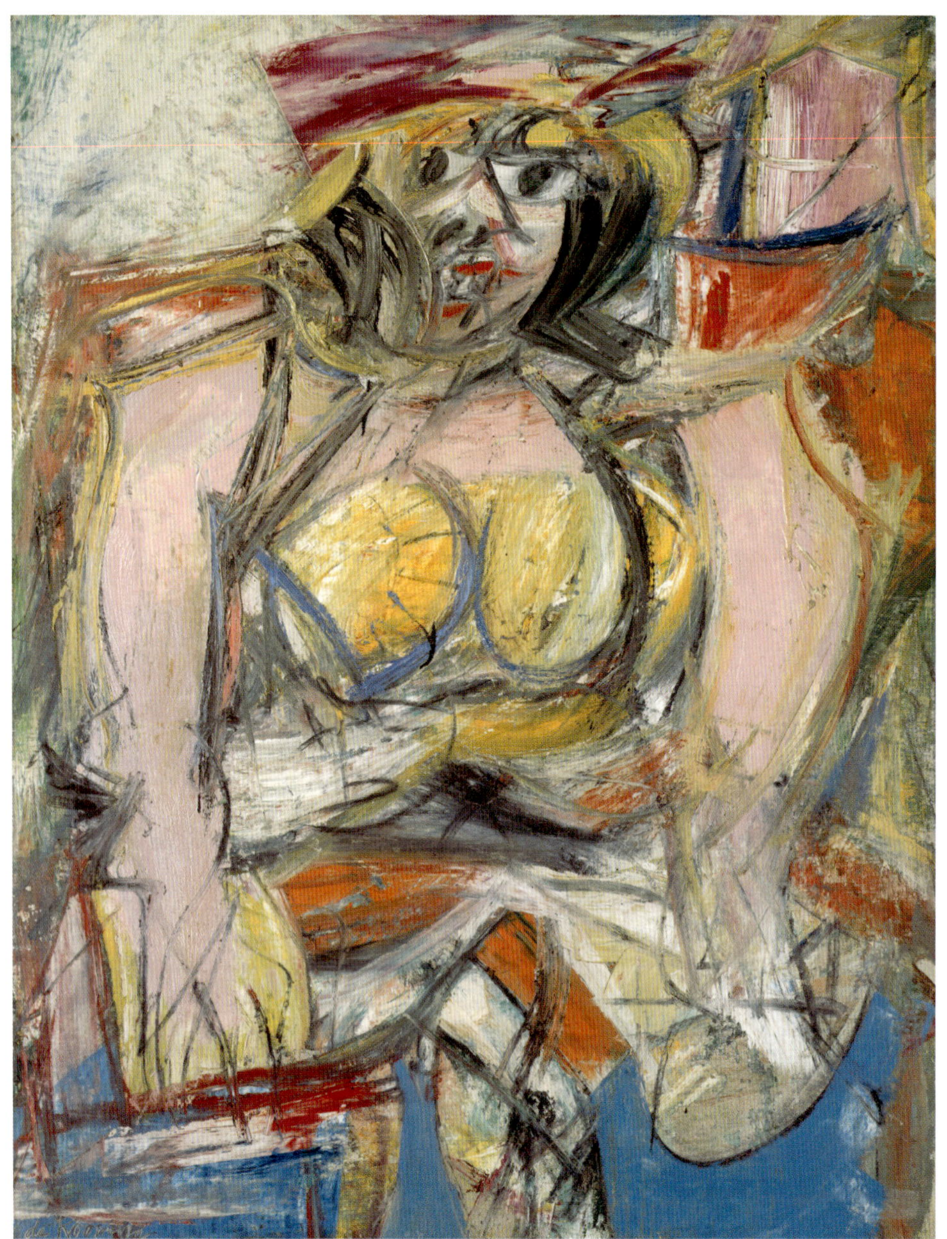

WILLEM DE KOONING,
American (b. The Netherlands,
1904–1997).
Woman IV, 1952–1953.
Oil, enamel, and charcoal on canvas.
Gift of William Inge, 56-128.

ROBERT RAUSCHENBERG,
American (b. 1925).
Tracer, 1963.
Oil and silkscreen on canvas.
Purchase, F84-70.

African

52

Beaded Throne,
19th century,
African, Cameroon, Bamileke
Chiefdom of Bansoa.
Wood, glass beads, shells, and fiber.
Purchase: Nelson Trust through the
George H. and Elizabeth O. Davis
Fund, 92-13.

Commemorative Head of an Oba,
16th century,
African, Nigeria, Benin Kingdom.
Brass.
Purchase: Nelson Trust through the
generosity of Donald J. and Adele C.
Hall, Mr. and Mrs. Herman Robert
Sutherland, and an anonymous
donor; The Nelson Gallery
Foundation; and the exchange of a
Trust property, 87-7.

Royal Stool,
ca. 1860,
African, Ghana, Asante peoples.
Wood and silver.
Purchase: Nelson Trust, 65-5.

Visitors move into the Helzberg Family Galleries, which feature an
African art collection that is distinguished by works that were chosen
for high artistic achievement rather than for anthropological
importance. The gallery features towering glass casework specially
designed to exhibit the works of art.

Photography

To the east is the Hallmark Cards Galleries, featuring the Hallmark Photographic Collection that surveys the history of this medium, from daguerreotypes and dry plates to the most contemporary digital works.

A doorway between the African galleries and photography galleries takes visitors to the featured exhibition space, the H&R Block Galleries, with flexibility to host large exhibitions. In the southwest corner of the building, the visitor is tantalized by a glimpse of the cubic gallery, a 34-foot cube that creates a geometric installation space.

DOROTHEA LANGE,
American (1895–1965).
Migrant Mother, Nipomo, California, 1936.
Gelatin silver print.
Gift of Hallmark Cards, Inc.,
P5.143.034.92.

UNKNOWN MAKER,
American,
The Daguerreotypist, ca. 1850.
Daguerreotype, half plate.
Gift of Hallmark Cards, Inc.,
P5.400.93.97.

The interior journey of the Bloch Building culminates at the Isamu Noguchi Sculpture Court. The space is named for Nelson-Atkins supporters Tinka and Harry McCray. The interior floors are of peribonka granite, polished to shine like a cool lake. A rock bed begins inside and emerges outside, into the exterior Noguchi Plaza, dissolving the separation between the gallery space and the outside world. The lush green grass of the Kansas City Sculpture Park meets the clear glass and seems to merge with the granite floors. The Isamu Noguchi Sculpture Court captures the essence of Holl's philosophy about the coming together of architecture and landscape. From this interior oasis, looking across the lawn to the grandeur of the original Nelson-Atkins, the visitor can observe the quiet simplicity of nature and the stately presence of the 1933 building.

Looking north, the fluid path of the gallery walk takes visitors past the galleries from which they just emerged. As visitors head up the gallery walk, a glass door provides an exit into the Kansas City Sculpture Park where more than 30 sculptures are installed. This door, one of eight throughout the two Museum buildings, encourages visitors to enter and exit as they please, creating a sense of porosity throughout the space.

GALLERY SPACES
(Left and right top) The interior spaces of the Bloch Building offer glimpses of galleries and of the Kansas City Sculpture Park just outside.
(Above) The Isamu Noguchi Sculpture Court, shown in this rendering, offers visitors a reflective space near the south end of the Bloch Building.

UNFOLDING
(Left) The Bloch Building lenses follow the natural slope of the Kansas City Sculpture Park.
(Below) The southern-most lenses, as seen in this view looking north from within the Sculpture Park.

Outdoor paths beckon visitors to explore the top of the Bloch Building. A gentle slope follows the rise of the south lawn, past Ursula von Rydingsvard's rugged *Three Bowls*, and to an elevated vantage point from between the two southern-most lenses. Here, Tony Cragg's organically shaped sculptures, *Ferryman* and *Turbo*, are juxtaposed against the linear glass panels of the Bloch Building. Visitors find themselves walking on a grassy topography that is created by the galleries and public spaces of the Bloch Building below. Here the blending of building and the Kansas City Sculpture Park becomes tangible. The path leads visitors between lenses, across a zig-zag path, now with a view of the original building and the East Sculpture Terrace.

From this vantage point atop the Bloch Building at the eastern edge of the Kansas City Sculpture Park, looking across the lush landscape and to the Country Club Plaza beyond, visitors can see the complete vision—the efforts in the early part of the 20th century to create a grand Museum, and the efforts in the early 21st century to build on that effort for generations to come.

ILLUMINATION
(Above) Two Tony Cragg sculptures from atop the Bloch Building are silhouetted by the glow of the lenses.

Tony Cragg, English (b. 1949). *Ferryman* (detail), 1997. Bronze. Acquired through the generosity of the Hall Family Foundation. 2001.26.1.

Turbo, 2001. Bronze. Acquired through the generosity of the Hall Family Foundation. 2001.26.2.

ROCKY CLIFFS
(Right) Sited at the south end of the Bloch Building, the sculpture *Three Bowls* stands tall in the Kansas City Sculpture Park.

Ursula von Rydingsvard, American (b. Germany, 1942). *Three Bowls*, 1990. Cedar and graphite. Purchase: Acquired through the generosity of the Hall Family Foundation, the George H. and Elizabeth O. Davis Fund, G. Kenneth Baum, and Judy and Alan Kosloff. 99-9 A-C.

INNER PASSAGE
Bronze figures from the sculpture
Rush Hour seem to emerge from
between the two buildings.

George Segal, American (1924–2000).
Rush Hour, 1983; cast 1995. Bronze. Gift
of the Hall Family Foundation. F99-
33/75 A-F

The Nelson-Atkins Museum of Art

4525 Oak Street, Kansas City, MO 64111-1873

Building Committee

Trustees
Harry McCray, Chairman
Henry Bloch, first Chairman
Rose Bryant
Charles Duboc
William Dunn Sr.
Richard Green Jr. (former)

Donald Hall
Shirley Helzberg
Ellen Hockaday
Richard Levin
Richard Owen
Estelle Sosland
James Sunderland

Staff
Dana Knapp
Barbara Justus
Marc Wilson
Karen Christiansen

Architectural Design Oversight Committee

Marc Wilson, *Director, Chair*
Dana Knapp, *Director of Planning, Project Director*
Barbara Justus, *Associate, Planning*
Elisabeth Batchelor, *Director, Conservation
    and Collections Management*
Ann Brubaker, *Director, Educational Affairs (retired)*
Stan Chandler, *Director, Operations*
Karen Christiansen, *Chief Operating Officer*
Michelle Lehrman Jenness, *Manager, Security & Visitor Services*
Deborah Emont Scott, *Chief Curator*
Steve Waterman, *Director, Design*
Rebecca Young, *Manager, Exhibition Design*
Mark Zimmerman, *Director, Visitor Services*
Henry Bloch, *Trustee*
Donald Hall, *Trustee*
Casey Cassias, *BNIM Architects*
Jim Lacy, *Lacy & Company*
Peter Lacy, *Lacy & Company*

Project Team

Program Manager: Lacy & Company, Kansas City, Missouri

Design Architect: Steven Holl
Partner in Charge: Chris McVoy, Steven Holl Architects,
    New York, New York
Associate Architect: BNIM Architects, Kansas City, Missouri
Lighting Design: Renfro Design Group, Inc., New York,
    New York
Landscape Architect: Gould Evans Goodman Associates,
    Kansas City, Missouri
Mechanical, Electrical & Plumbing Engineer: Ove Arup &
    Partners, New York, New York
Associate Mechanical, Electrical & Plumbing Engineer:
    W.L. Cassell & Associates Inc., Kansas City, Missouri
Structural Engineer: Guy Nordenson & Associates,
    New York, New York
Associate Structural Engineer: Structural Engineering
    Associates, Kansas City, Missouri

General Contractor: J.E. Dunn Construction Company,
    Kansas City Missouri

Board of Trustees – FY '93-Present

Mary Atterbury	Ann Dickinson	Donald Hall	Richard Levin	Dolph Simons Jr.
Kenneth Baum	Charles Duboc	Paul Henson	Alan Marsh	Louis Smith
Robert Bernstein	William Dunn Sr.	Ellen Hockaday	Harry McCray	Estelle Sosland
Henry Bloch	Laura Fields	Shirley Helzberg	Thomas McDonnell	James Sunderland
Rose Bryant	Gary Forsee	Stephanie Jacobson	John McMeel	Herman Sutherland
Thornton Cooke II	Scott Francis	Laurence Jones	Fred Merrill	Helen Jane Uhlmann
Paul Copaken	Ollie Gates	Julia Irene Kauffman	John Palmer	Adelaide Ward
Ilus Davis	Richard Green Jr.	Leonard Kline	George Powell	
Paul DeBruce	Mary Ann Hale	Len Lauer	Sarah Rowland	

First published in 2007 by
Scala Publishers
Northburgh House
10 Northburgh Street
London EC1V 0AT
www.scalapublishers.com
Tel: 00 44 20 7490 9900

The Nelson-Atkins Museum of Art
4525 Oak Street
Kansas City, Missouri 64111
www.nelson-atkins.org
Tel: 816-751-1278

Distributed in the booktrade by
Antique Collectors' Club Limited
Eastworks
116 Pleasant Street, Suite 60B
Easthampton, Massachusetts 01027

ISBN-10: 1-85759-482-7
ISBN-13: 978-1-85759-482-9

10 9 8 7 6 5 4 3 2 1

Project Manager: Lara Kline
Text: Toni Wood, Ann Slegman
Editor: Esme West
Designer: Nigel Soper
Illustration of glass system: Zhon Champie
Map design: Barbara Worthington
Image Assistance: Michele and Joseph Boeckholt
Produced by Scala Publishers
Printed and bound in Hong Kong

Photographic Credits